12/02

03
11

09

ILL40
1

ILL09
1

12/02

contemporary
painted furniture

contemporary
painted furniture

Katrin Cargill

photography by David Montgomery

painting by Tabby Riley

RYLAND
PETERS
& SMALL

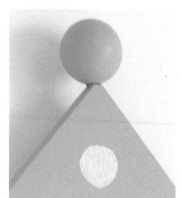

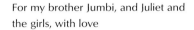

For my brother Jumbi, and Juliet and
the girls, with love

Publishing director	Anne Ryland
Designer	Victoria Holmes
Assistant designer	Sailesh Patel
Design consultant	Meryl Lloyd
Editor	Maddalena Bastianelli
Editorial manager	Sian Parkhouse
Artist	Tabby Riley
Stylist	Katrin Cargill
Production	Patricia Harrington

First published in Great Britain in 1999 by
Ryland Peters & Small, Cavendish House,
51–55 Mortimer Street, London W1N 7TD

10 9 8 7 6 5 4 3 2 1

ISBN 1 900518 75 9

A catalogue record for this book is available from
the British Library.

Printed and bound in China by Toppan Printing Co.

contents

from the beginning

For centuries painters around the world have
left their mark on furniture, from elaborately
gilded pastoral scenes on mirrors to plain
numerals on school chairs. There is nothing
new about painted furniture – indeed there are
many books on how to recreate traditional
paint effects – but with the emergence of more
pared-down interiors today, coupled with a
growing selection of flat-packed and unfinished
furniture now available, I feel there is a need
for a simpler approach to this craft. For this
book I have drawn on techniques and ideas
from the past; patterns from everyday items;
even natural surroundings have influenced
several projects. Painting furniture is fun and
you don't need to be an artist to have a go. Be
inspired by colours, patterns and objects that
you really love – don't be afraid to experiment.

Colour schemes can be determined with the aid of old textiles: this collection of red, white and stone-grey Irish linen influenced my choice of colours and decoration for the kitchen (*see pages 46-60*).

This antique patchwork quilt is highly decorated, but on closer inspection its pattern is quite simple. The geometric star in the centre was the inspiration behind the sunburst bathroom shelf on page 90.

gathering ideas

Flea markets and junk shops make great hunting ground for ideas. The mix of light blue, indigo and white on these tin cups provided the inspiration for the crested garland box on page 78.

Flowers are probably the most commonly used motifs on painted furniture. Petals have a geometric perfection which suits stencilling and stamping in a repeating fashion.

Polka dots have such a jolly appeal. They fall into that rare category of simple but chic, earthy yet elegant. This blue pot from the Haute-Savoie in France gave me the idea of painting gold dots on a candle sconce (*see page 22*).

Botanical themes offer a huge source of inspiration. The pattern of falling leaves on this cool-coloured ceramic soap dish evokes feelings of light summer evenings.

The colours and patterns in this section are inspired by the palette of Scandinavia: pale aqua blues, greys and greens. The patterns are easy to achieve and the techniques vary from printing with a sponge roller to rustic wood graining. All the ideas can be adapted to different sizes and styles of furniture by scaling up or down.

eating and

entertaining

dining table
folk flowers

materials

Wooden dining table

Lichen green and pale green water-based eggshell paint

Egg-yolk yellow and dark green concentrated artist's acrylic colour

Household paint brush

Soft leaded pencil

Metal ruler

Masking tape, low-tack

White conté pastel, sharpened

Black permanent marker pen

Sponge roller refill

Craft knife

Flat oil-based varnish, extra pale

Varnishing brush

preparation

Table should be sanded, acrylic primer undercoat applied and painted with 2 coats of green water-based eggshell paint

This simple repeating stylized motif takes its inspiration from the painted exteriors of rural Norwegian farmsteads. The cheerful naive painting on window frames, shutters and doors, usually in just one or two colours, lends itself well to furniture. Here, a pine country table is painted in a soft cool lichen green, with a panel of paler green in the centre. An egg-yolk yellow flower motif is printed with a cut-out sponge, and then outlined in a darker green to accentuate the pattern. The flowers are printed around the aproned sides of the table as well. The central decorated panel still looks pretty even when the table is laid. Colour is all important here; the brightness and depth of the yellow paint is what give this very simple pattern its strength. A paler yellow would get lost in the greens. If you decide to use colours that will suit your decorating scheme, remember that the flower motif should be strong and bright, and the table colours more receding and muted.

dining chairs
swedish flowers

materials

Wooden chairs

Blue water-based eggshell paint

Pale blue and ivory concentrated artist's acrylic colour

Household paint brush

Tracing paper

Soft leaded pencil

Masking tape, low-tack

Fine-tipped artist's brush

Clear matt acrylic varnish

Varnishing brush

preparation

Chairs should be sanded, acrylic primer undercoat applied and painted with 2 coats of blue water-based eggshell paint

Scandinavia is the European home for rural painted furniture. So many wonderful pieces exist in the many living museums that it is hard not to be inspired by their charming ideas. These pretty Swedish-style chairs need little embellishment and for this reason I have kept the pattern very simple: just a two-colour motif across the back slats. The beauty is in the strong cool blue base colour of the chair coupled with the lighter blues of the pattern. There are many inexpensive unpainted chairs available, often rather crude looking in unfinished wood. The transformation by paint is so satisfying, you'll soon be infected by enthusiasm. If you have a motley assortment of dining chairs collected over the years, in different colours, woods, or shapes, you can paint them all and transform them into a handsome set. For fun, the pattern is echoed in the seat cushions also. The garland pattern has been slightly adapted to fit the cushion, and painted with colourfast fabric paint onto a subtle checked blue cotton fabric.

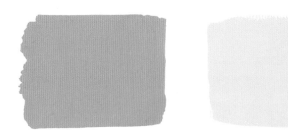

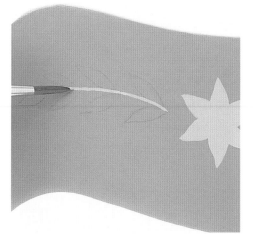

1 Transfer motif to chair back

Trace the motif (see page 120) onto tracing paper. Tape the tracing paper onto the crossbar of the chair so the pencil lines face down and transfer the image by drawing over the design with a pencil. Remove the paper and retrace any faint lines.

2 Paint petals

Using pale blue paint, colour in the petals with a fine-tipped brush. Remember to paint slightly over the pencil outline to cover it up.

3 Paint Stems

Following the pencil guidelines, paint fine stems running between the flowers using pale blue paint. Remember to paint over the pencil lines to cover them up.

5 Add ivory dot to centre of flowers

For the top rail, enlarge the flower motif on a photocopier so that the flower will sit comfortably on the chair back. Trace the motif, apply it to the chair back and paint as before. Dot ivory paint in the centre of each flower. Apply 2 coats of varnish to finish.

4 Add leaves to stems

Paint the leaves using pale blue paint, making sure you go over the pencil lines. Allow to dry.

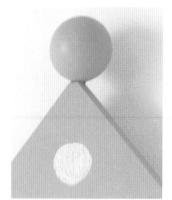

candle sconce
gold leaf dots

materials

Wooden candle sconce

Grey-green water-based satinwood paint

Household paint brush

White conté pastel, sharpened

Metal ruler

Button, coin or washer with 2 cm diameter

Hard-tipped artist's brush

gold leaf paint

preparation

Sconce should be sanded, acrylic primer undercoat applied and painted with 2 coats of grey-green water-based satinwood paint

Gilding has formed the backbone of paint decorated furniture for centuries. Think of the countless gilded mirrors, picture frames and ornate furniture – lovely in the appropriate setting, but in a more pared-down interior all that gold can be too much. Swedish interiors seem to make gold work. Their secret is in using very little of it, and mixing it with lots of plain flat colour. One of the prettiest effects often seen in Swedish dining rooms is in their use of candle light reflected in mirrors, or gilded wall brackets. This modern wooden candle sconce emulates this effect with the use of gold leaf paint. When the candles are lit the light dances and reflects off the golden dots. The secret with gold leaf and silver leaf is in its subtlety – a little goes a long way; just the odd glimmer of gold can look magical in evening light. To determine the size of the gold dots, try different sized coins or washers, by outlining in conté pastel, and seeing if the size suits the scale of the sconce.

1 Draw parallel lines

Mark conté pastel dots along each side of
the sconce about 1 cm in from the edge.
Join up the dots to create a line all around
the edge of the sconce. Repeat for the
second line, this time about 3 cm in from
the edge.

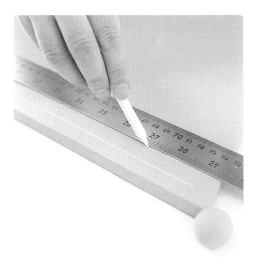

3 Paint gold circles

Paint in the circles with
gold leaf paint using a
hard-tipped artist's
brush. Allow to dry.
Rub out the white
pastel lines.

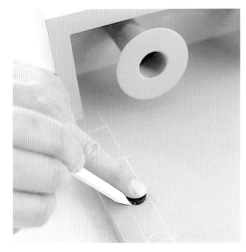

2 Draw around button

Mark a dot at the bottom of each side of the
sconce, about 2 cm up from the base, then
mark dots 4 cm apart. Draw a horizontal
line through each dot, put a button or coin
over each line and draw around it.

hanging shelf
rustic graining

materials

MDF shelf

Cream oil-based eggshell paint

Household paint brush

Decorator's tape

Oil-based scumble glaze

Olive green artist's oil paint

Stippling brush or dusting brush

Lint-free cotton cloth

Rubber-ended brush with wedged tip

Flat oil-based varnish, extra pale

Varnishing brush

preparation

Shelf should be sanded, acrylic primer undercoat applied and painted with 2 coats of cream oil-based eggshell paint

A quirky paint effect for a quirky hanging shelf! Wood graining has been around for a long time, usually seen on soft and cheaper wood to make it look more expensive or unusual. Good wood graining cannot be distinguished from the real thing. Often painters would not know what woods looked like so they would invent their own interpretation, and many examples of this can be seen on rural painted furniture such as trunks and chests. But to me the charm of a more naive and fanciful graining is very attractive. The pattern created is crude, rough and wonderful – the lovely thing about this graining technique is that you don't need years of training and you can create your own pattern as you go along. However, because you have to stipple and grain over wet paint, you need a certain amount of speed and dexterity, so practise first on scrap wood or card. It is important to work on one section of the shelf at a time and allow it to dry thoroughly before moving onto the next part. Drying time will be long when using an oil-based medium.

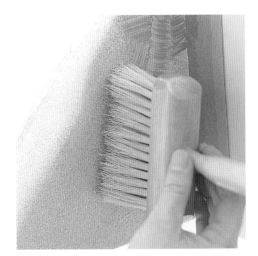

1 Apply tinted scumble glaze

Tint the scumble glaze to a desired depth of colour with the olive green paint. Using a household brush, paint the tinted scumble onto a masked-off section of shelf.

2 Stipple painted surface

While the tinted scumble is still wet, use a stippling brush to stipple the painted surface. It is easier to control the stippling if you hold the brush upright and grasp it at the base of the handle. Remove the tape.

3 Wipe edges clean of paint

Using a damp lint-free cotton cloth, wipe off any excess scumble that may have gone over the edge of the painted area – this will give the edge a neat, clean base on which to apply the tinted scumble later.

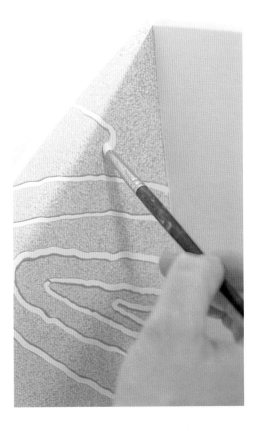

4 Imitate wood grain

Using a rubber-ended brush with a wedged tip, add swirling patterns in the wet scumble to loosely imitate wood grain. Hold the brush lightly so that you can achieve slightly uneven lines. Wipe the excess scumble off the brush with a cloth as you go along. Remember to bring the lines over the edge of the shelf to continue the wood grain effect. Allow this section of the shelf to dry. Repeat the masking, painting, stippling and line drawing process for the inside of the other vertical strut.

5 Continue wood theme

Mask off the top shelf and paint, stipple and draw in lines as before. Change the angle of the line as you turn the edge to match the vertical struts. Repeat for the other shelves and the outside of the struts. Allow to dry. Apply 2 coats of varnish to finish.

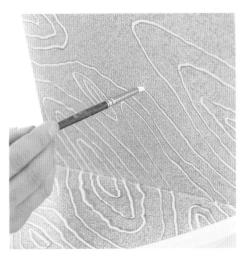

enhance with cool tones and

Accessories painted the same colour unify items in a room, like these pale grey candlesticks and a wooden tray.

A pine country serving table has been given a wash of watered-down paint: grey-blue for the top and white for the base. Diluted colours will give a large piece of furniture a light and contemporary feel, especially when used in a pale colour scheme.

pale washes

A pair of classical Swedish dining chairs painted traditional Scandinavian grey are complemented by the red country check of the seat cushions. This shade of grey is cool and sophisticated, which enhances the elegant shape of the chairs. Using a subtle, unobtrusive colour such as grey in the background allows stronger colours to stand happily in front.

This section contains a diverse selection of old painting tricks interpreted in a modern way. Traditional methods, such as mosaic and comb painting are used on modern, simple pieces of furniture to create a cool, contemporary look in the living room.

unwind

and relax

wooden sofa
combed squares

materials

Wooden sofa

Buttermilk water-based
eggshell paint

Large household paint brush

Metal ruler

Yellow ochre coloured pencil

Decorator's tape

Window cleaner's squeegee,
from which 1 cm wedges have
been cut out

Craft knife

Acrylic scumble glaze

Yellow ochre concentrated
artist's acrylic colour

Dark ochre concentrated
artist's acrylic colour

Square-ended artist's brush

Clear matt acrylic varnish

Varnishing brush

preparation

Woodwork should be sanded,
acrylic primer undercoat
applied and painted with
2 coats of buttermilk
water-based eggshell paint

Combing is a traditional American decorating technique used by folk artists in the 18th century to create patterns by dragging a combing tool through a glaze. The principle remains the same today, but a modern look can be created by exaggerating the process to dramatic effect with wavy lines, zigzags, checks or swirling patterns. Here, the geometric pattern of wavy lines has turned a plain wooden sofa into a striking piece of furniture. Colour combinations are endless; using a dark tinted glaze over a pale background will look more attractive than a light colour on top of a dark one. Using a water-based scumble glaze reduces the lengthy drying time associated with an oil-based glaze. The clever use of a window cleaner's squeegee to make a combing tool means that you don't need to spend a lot of money on specialist equipment. It also means that you can cut out the comb's 'teeth' to a width of your choice.

1 Mark out squares

Divide each side of the sofa into squares, about 25 cm each (or as square as possible given the dimensions of the sofa). Using a pencil in a similar colour to the scumble, mark out squares with the ruler.

2 Mask off squares

Using decorator's tape, mask off rows of alternate squares – these are the squares you will paint first. Put a piece of tape in the centre of the squares to be painted later – this will prevent you from inadvertently painting them.

3 Paint squares

Tint the scumble to a desired depth of colour with the yellow ochre paint. Using a large paint brush, apply the tinted scumble in long even vertical brush strokes. You must not paint adjoining squares at the same time or the scumble will run.

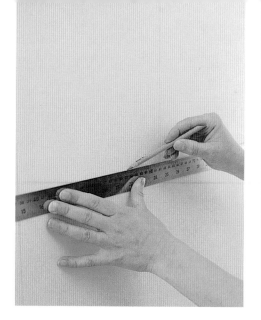

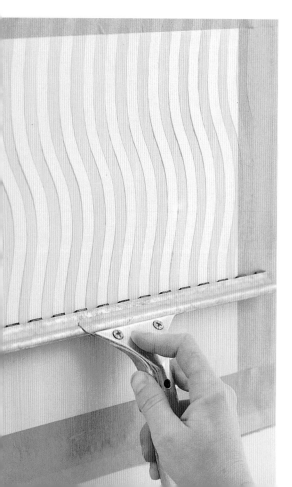

4 Comb scumbled squares

For vertical wavy lines start at the top of the square and drag the comb steadily through the tinted scumble to the bottom, moving the comb from side to side as you go. For even lines, it is best to drag the comb through the scumble in one fluid movement. Remove the tape and allow to dry.

5 Vertical-lined squares

Repeat the masking, painting and combing for all the vertical squares on alternate rows, remembering to put a tape marker in the centre of the alternate squares to paint in horizontal lines later. Remove the tape surrounding each finished square and allow to dry. Repeat for all the remaining vertical squares on the sofa.

6 Horizontal-lined squares

Mask off the horizontal squares that do not touch along alternate rows. Remove the markers on the squares you have masked. Apply the tinted scumble, working on one square at a time as before, but this time with horizontal brush strokes. Drag the comb through the scumble as before, but this time up and down from left to right to create horizontal wavy lines. Remove the tape. Allow to dry. Repeat the process for all the sides of the sofa for the first set of horizontal squares.

7 Alternating horizontals

Once the scumble has dried, mask off the remaining horizontal squares in the alternate rows. (Remove the marker tapes before painting.) Working on one square at at a time, apply the tinted scumble and create horizontal wavy lines as before. Repeat for each side of the sofa. Remove the decorator's tape and allow to dry.

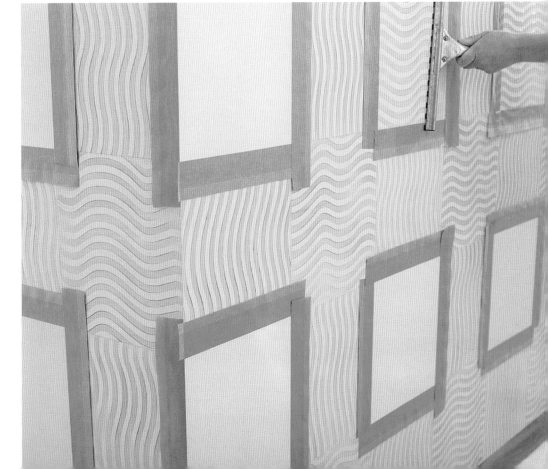

8 Paint edges of sofa

Using a square-ended artist's brush and
dark ochre, hand-paint the edges to give
the sofa a neat finish. Allow to dry. Apply
2 coats of varnish to finish.

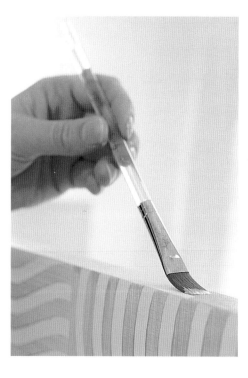

coffee table
broad stripes

materials

Wooden coffee table

Coarse- and fine-grade sandpaper

Masking tape

Large household paint brush

Concentrated artist's acrylic colour in light ochre and plum, diluted with water

Satin oil-based varnish

Varnishing brush

preparation

Table should be sanded – if the surface is rough, first sand it with coarse-grade sandpaper then finish with fine-grade

A coffee table is a useful piece of living room furniture, which is given centre stage in most homes so style, size, shape, design, colour and material are all important. With this in mind, coffee tables make the perfect medium for painting and decorating. Colourwashing is an age-old technique which is as popular today as it has ever been. Its beauty lies in the subtle colour treatment which allows the natural grain and textures of wood to show through and for best results, should be used on soft wood or wood which has been sandblasted to absorb colour. Make sure you smooth the masking tape down well, to section off the panels; this will stop the colour from one panel merging into another. Afterwards, use a strong oil-based varnish to seal the wood. Coffee tables can be notoriously heavy to move but here attaching wheels to the legs overcomes this back-wrenching problem to become part of the table's overall modern appeal. You can complement this contemporary setting with the up-to-the-minute combed sofa on page 32.

1 Section off panels with tape

Following the natural lines on the planks of wood which make up the table top, mask off 4 unequal panels; take the masking tape over the edge of the table.

3 Paint plum acrylic panels

Mask off the remaining alternate panels as before. Using a large paint brush and diluted plum acrylic, paint the panels on the top and edges of the table. Remove the tape. Allow to dry. Apply 2 coats of varnish to finish.

2 Paint ochre acrylic panels

Using a large paint brush and diluted light ochre acrylic, fill in 2 alternate masked-off panels, remembering to paint over the edges of the table. Remove the tape. Allow to dry.

large mirror
modern mosaic

materials

Wooden framed mirror

Decorator's tape

Cream water-based satinwood paint

Household paint brush

Soft leaded pencil

Metal ruler

Plastic ruler

Concentrated artist's acrylic colour in light olive, umber, terracotta, soft pink and pale umber

Square-ended artist's brush

Clear matt acrylic varnish

Varnishing brush

preparation

Frame of mirror should be sanded; mirror masked off with decorator's tape; acrylic primer undercoat applied to frame and painted with 2 coats of cream water-based satinwood paint

This uncluttered room needs little besides a magnificent mosaic floor standing mirror. Mosaic has a wonderfully timeless and peaceful appeal, especially when earthy colours are used. The painted mirror looks like a labour of love, but it is only the accurate measuring and marking out of the squares that requires most attention. The painting itself is not as perfect as it first appears; in fact the pattern benefits from the slightly imperfect or rough edges achieved from freehand painting. This is a project that can be worked on at your leisure – you could take two days from start to finish or you could dip in and out of it as you might do with knitting or embroidery.

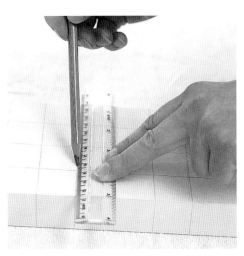

1 Draw lines along frame

Work out how many 2.5 cm squares you can fit in the frame of the mirror. (If the frame does not divide exactly, size the squares accordingly.) Using a pencil and ruler, draw in parallel lines 2.5 cm apart from top to bottom and down the sides of the frame.

2 Finish squares

Once the parallel lines have been drawn in on all sides of the frame, add vertical lines 2.5 cm apart on all sides of the frame to complete the squares, remembering to take the pencil lines over the edge of the frame and down the sides.

3 Apply first colour

Using a square-ended artist's brush and working with one colour at a time, paint one square in every six light olive, taking the paint right up to the edge of the pencil lines. Don't forget to paint the outer and inner squares of the frame edge.

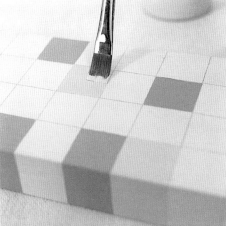

5 Complete squares

Continue to fill one square in every six, for the remaining three colours. Allow the last set of squares to dry. Apply 2 coats of varnish to finish.

4 Apply second colour

Let the light olive squares dry before moving on to another colour. Using soft pink paint and the same brush, which has been washed and dried, paint in the next set of squares.

emphasize elegance with light

The faintest shade of yellow paint on this regal-looking mirror enhances and defines its delicate shape.

The linear design of this elegant wooden cot sofa brings furniture into a contemporary dimension. Checks do not seem to date, and when used for soft furnishings, they are always stylish and fresh.

colours

Pale, plain and unobtrusive, this softly painted lamp base with a square
card shade does not dominate the small side table.

cooking

Kitchen furniture is ideal for painting – built-in cupboards, dressers, tables and chairs take on a fresh look – even wooden floors can be given a new lease of life. Pattern ideas are taken from tea towels, gingham fabric and the more unusual floral print of a Japanese kimono.

and storing

storage cupboard
kimono flowers

materials

Wooden cupboard

Red water-based satinwood paint

Cream water-based satinwood paint

Household paint brushes

Self-adhesive stickers

Acetate

Black permanent marker pen

Craft knife

Cutting mat

White conté pastel, sharpened

Masking tape, low-tack

Dark red and cream concentrated artist's acrylic colour

Square-ended artist's brush

Fine-tipped artist's brush

Clear matt acrylic varnish

Varnishing brush

preparation

Cupboard should be sanded; acrylic primer undercoat applied; outside painted red, inside and shelves painted cream, using 2 coats of water-based satinwood paint

Storage is the key to an organized and practical kitchen, and this large open fronted cupboard can hold a large amount of crockery, glassware and kitchenware. The inspiration for this stencilled floral pattern was an antique Japanese kimono – I took a small flower motif from a complex pattern and created a layered stencil (see template on page 124). The design is refreshingly simple, and painting flowers randomly onto the outside of the cupboard not only breaks up the solid block of red but gives the appearance of the flowers tumbling down the sides. The flowers are confined to the exterior of the cupboard only, to give the inside an uncluttered appearance. In an otherwise creamy coloured kitchen, warm red adds a splash of colour. The light interior of the cupboard gives the illusion of more space as well as complementing the cream china on the shelves. It is easy to create stencils from your own design or from other sources and I have explained clearly on page 118 how this can be achieved.

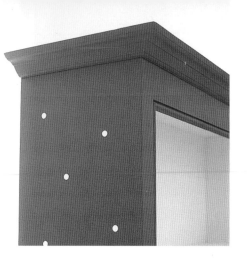

1 Mark position guides

Put self-adhesive stickers at random onto both sides of the cupboard to mark the position for each flower. Copy the stencils (see page 124), scaling up or down as required. Trace onto acetate and include registration marks. Cut out using a craft knife and cutting mat.

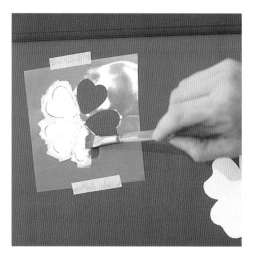

3 Paint in petalled stencil

Position the second stencil (the petalled flower) over a sticker, as for the first stencil, and paint in cream acrylic. Repeat, stencilling at random over several stickers on both sides of the cupboard. Wipe the stencil clean and use for the remaining stickers, this time painting in red acrylic. Allow to dry.

2 Draw in registration marks

Tape the first stencil (the solid flower outline) over one sticker, then remove the sticker. Mark through the registration holes. Using a square-ended brush, fill in the stencil with cream acrylic. Lift off the stencil and repeat, stencilling in a random pattern over several stickers.

4 Stencil petals over flower

Put the second stencil (the petalled flower) over a solid cream flower, making sure the registration marks align with the original conté pastel marks. Fill in the stencil with red acrylic. Carefully remove stencil. Repeat, stencilling on top of the other solid cream flowers. Allow to dry.

5 Add flower details

Using a fine-tipped brush, add details to each flower design as follows: For the cream-petalled flowers – dot the centre with cream acrylic and add short red lines to each petal. For the red-petalled flowers – dot the centre with cream acrylic and add short cream lines to each petal. For the cream flowers with red petals – dot the centre with red and add short cream lines to each petal. Allow to dry.
For the front panel of the cupboard, find its centre and stencil in a cream flower with red petals, then stencil a cream-petalled flower either side of it. You may need to scale down the size of the stencils to fit. Allow to dry. Apply 2 coats of varnish to the inside and outside of the cupboard to finish.

spice cabinet
painted gingham

materials

Wooden, glass-fronted wall cabinet

Decorator's tape

Water-based satinwood paint in light stone, ivory and stone

Household paint brush

White conté pastel, sharpened

Ruler

Masking tape, low tack

Graph paper

Black permanent marker pen

Acetate

Craft knife

Cutting mat

Spray adhesive

Square-ended artist's brush

Clear matt acrylic varnish

Varnishing brush

preparation

Cabinet should be sanded, glass panes masked off with decorator's tape, acrylic primer undercoat applied and painted with 2 coats of light-stone water-based satinwood paint

Gingham has such a timeless and fresh appeal that it is both naive and sophisticated. Interpreting it into a paint effect is most attractive. The checked pattern is created by the weaving of two colours; the third colour is created where the two colours overlap. (Bear this in mind if you decide to use different colours.) As with all striped patterns or chequerboard patterns, the key to success lies in the preparation and marking out stage. Working out the size and scale of the pattern is important but the ingenious use of a square-gridded stencil will facilitate painting. If you look closely at the squares that make up the finished pattern, you will see that they occasionally overlap a little. It is this slight overlap that gives the paint effect charm as well as a realistic appearance of fabric weave. The inside of the cabinet is stencilled in larger squares to provide a contrast to the outside. Also, it is less tricky to paint large squares within the confined space of a cabinet.

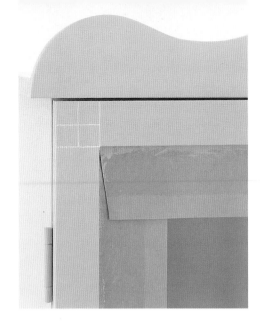

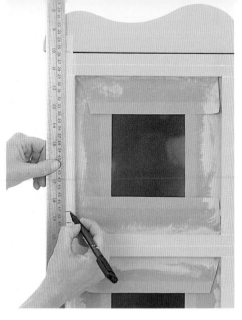

1 Square off cabinet corners

Draw a square at each corner of the cabinet and either side of each crossbar on the door, then divide into 4 smaller squares, about 2.5 cm each. This will make marking out the rest of the cabinet more accurate. Join the large squares by drawing lines through the centre of each one.

2 Make a marker tape

To make a marker tape for the squares, put a strip of masking tape down one side of the cabinet front. Using a ruler and pen, mark out 2.5 cm intervals or intervals equivalent to the small squares already drawn at the corners. Use the tape and pastel to mark the front and join up to form parallel lines.

3 Draw horizontal lines

Using the marker tape and conté pastel, make marks down both edges of one side of the cabinet. Draw in parallel lines, joining up the marks, using a ruler for straight lines. Repeat the taping, marking and joining up process for the other side of the cabinet.

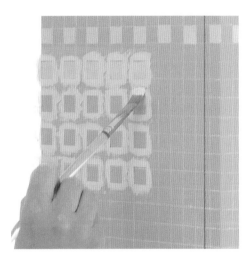

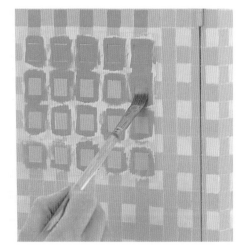

7 Cover side with squares

Reposition the stencil laying it on top of the grid, next to the first set of ivory squares and paint as before. Repeat on all the sides and front of the cabinet. Allow to dry.

8 Stencil stone squares

For the gingham effect, use the same stencil as before, but this time start with the stencil 2 lines down from the top and 2 columns in from the edge. Paint the squares stone. Repeat stone pattern on all sides of cabinet.

9 Paint top row of squares

Mask off the row of ivory squares around the top of the cabinet and paint in a row of alternate grey squares. Using a household paint brush, paint the pelmet stone. Remove masking and decorator's tape. Allow to dry.

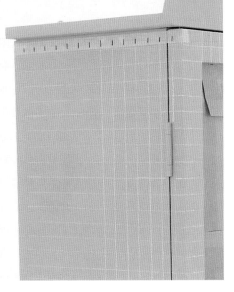

4 Draw vertical lines

Repeat the process for the vertical lines, but this time put the tape around the base of the cabinet and draw in marks using a conté pastel. Do the same around the top, then join up the marks from top to bottom to form a square grid.

5 Cut out a stencil of squares

On graph paper, draw a template of squares (the same size as the squares on the cabinet) and mark a cross in alternate squares on alternate rows. Tape acetate on top of the template. Using a craft knife and cutting mat, cut out the crossed squares.

6 Stencil ivory squares

Apply spray adhesive to the back of the stencil and leave for 30 seconds until tacky. Starting one line down from the top, put the stencil on top of the grid over the first column of squares. Paint in the ivory squares, then carefully lift off the stencil.

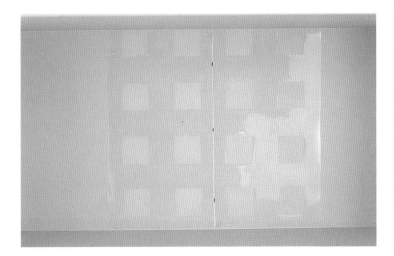

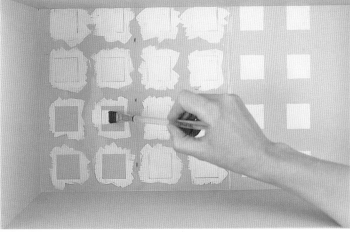

10 Find centre inside cabinet

Make a larger square stencil, as before, and draw positioning marks down the centre of the stencil. Find the centre inside the cabinet and draw a vertical line to mark this. Secure the stencil in place, laying the positioning marks on top of the white line. Paint in ivory squares.

11 Stencil inside cabinet

Continue to stencil large cream squares around the inside walls of the cabinet, followed by large stone squares, using the same method as on the outside. Allow to dry. Apply 2 coats of varnish, inside and outside, to finish.

kitchen table
tea towel motif

materials

*Polished steel-topped
wooden table*

*Cream water-based
satinwood paint*

Household paint brushes

Decorator's tape

Black permanent marker pen

T -square or ruler

Red coloured pencil

Masking tape

Metre ruler

Acrylic scumble glaze

*Red concentrated artist's
acrylic colour*

Flat oil-based varnish, extra pale

Varnishing brush

preparation

*Table should be sanded,
acrylic primer undercoat
applied and painted with
2 coats of cream water-based
satinwood paint*

Antique tea towels come in an assortment of weaves and patterns. They may be elaborately stitched with embroidery or plainly decorated with a simple weave. Either way, they are immensely collectable. Based on the simple crossed lines of a traditional Irish linen tea towel, a plain wooden work table with a practical polished-steel top is transformed into a fun, light and airy piece of furniture that would blend into virtually any modern kitchen. Its chunky square legs, bottom shelf and aproned sides provide an ideal surface for a simple motif like this one. For the translucent paint effect, which simulates the tea towel weave, scumble glaze is used, mixed with artist's acrylic colour. To achieve the most effective look, keep the base colour of the table white or ivory – the same as a tea towel – and stay with the traditional colours of red and white, blue and white or green and white.

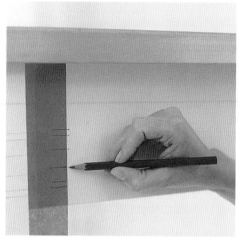

1 Mark out stripes on leg

Using a strip of decorator's tape the length of the table leg and a black pen, mark out groups of 3 stripes (like tea towel stripes) on the tape. Stick the marked tape on the edge of the table leg. Draw in horizontal lines at the pen marks using a T-square and red pencil.

2 Draw lines around leg

Remove the marker tape, then continue to draw in the stripes around the table leg – butt the T-square against the side of the leg and make sure it lines up with the first set of red pencil lines. Repeat steps 1 and 2 for the other legs.

3 Mark out front panel

Using the same marker tape as before and starting at one end of the table panel, make pencil marks to line up with the first group of lines at the top of the table leg. Continue to mark along the panel using the marker tape as a guide.

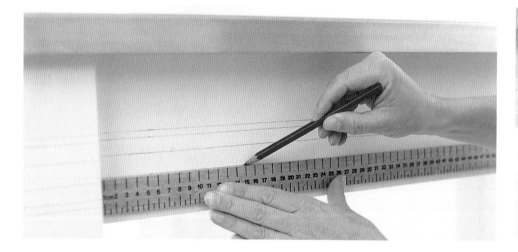

4 Draw parallel lines along front panel

Once all the marks have been made along the front panel, join them up. It is best to use a long ruler to join up the marks to achieve perfect lines. Repeat steps 3 and 4 on the remaining panels of the table. If the table has a bottom shelf, measure out, mark and draw in a group of horizontal lines along both lengths of it.

5 Mask off stripes

Using masking tape, mask off all the groups of horizontal stripes down the table legs, facing panels and bottom shelf. (Put the tape outside the pencil lines.)

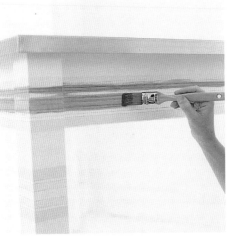

6 Paint red scumble lines

Tint the scumble glaze to a desired depth of colour with red acrylic and paint in the masked-off areas. Direct the brush strokes in one direction for a streaked effect. Remove the tape. Allow to dry, preferably overnight.

7 Cross-over lines

Mark out, mask and paint cross-over lines as before. Remove tape. Allow to dry. (Repeat for the bottom shelf so the cross-over lines match the panels.) Apply 2 coats of varnish.

serving tray
shaker bird

materials

Oval wooden tray, unvarnished

White conté pastel, sharpened

Craft knife

Medium-sized potato

Square-ended artist's brush

Red concentrated artist's acrylic colour

Varnishing brush

Acrylic liming paste

Lint-free cotton cloth

Fine wire wool (optional)

Flat oil-based varnish, extra pale

preparation

Tray should be clean, grease-free and sanded with fine sandpaper if neccessary

Liming is a very old paint treatment which was originally used on woodwork to accentuate the woodgrain and to give a chalky finish. It has seen a revival in recent years as a paint finish because its appeal is so natural and pure. The simple repetition of a one-colour motif works its own magic, particularly on small items such as this oval serving tray where the motif is the Shaker bird of peace. Potato printing is suprisingly easy and fun to do and will probably remind you of your childhood days when it was a favourite pastime.

4 Apply liming paste

Using a varnishing brush, paint a thin layer of liming paste over the surface of the tray covering the bird motifs as you go. You should still be able to see the bird design underneath.

1 Position bird cut-outs

Using a conté pastel, mark out a 5-cm border on the tray to represent the position guide for the cut-outs. Make 12 copies of the shaker bird template (see page 122) and cut them out. Lay the birds in pairs, head-to-head around the tray on the inside of the border.

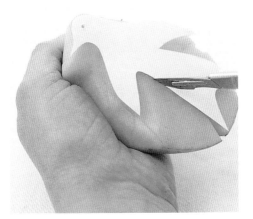

2 Cut around bird template

Cut a potato in half and press one bird cut-out onto the wet surface of the cut potato to stick. Using a craft knife, cut away around the cut-out to make a printing block and using the tip of the knife, pierce a hole in the potato to make the bird's eye.

3 Print onto tray surface

Dip the printing block into a saucer of red paint to coat. Remove a cut-out from the tray and print a red bird in its place. Press the printing block firmly onto the tray, lift it off and repeat for the remaining birds. (Recoat with paint as needed.) Allow to dry.

5 Work liming paste into tray

Rub down the tray all over with a soft, lint-free cotton cloth, working the cloth in a circular motion to achieve a bloomed effect. To give the tray a more distressed look, use wire wool to rub down the surface. Apply 2 coats of varnish to finish. Allow to dry.

add warmth with red painted

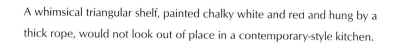

A whimsical triangular shelf, painted chalky white and red and hung by a thick rope, would not look out of place in a contemporary-style kitchen.

This rustic country-style egg rack is as practical as it is attractive; it has been varnished to withstand the rigours of kitchen life.

accessories

Old wooden spoon racks are a common antique shop or junk store find. The combination of straight and curved edges gives this three-tiered rack a unique appeal. The boldness of the red defines shape, making other forms of decoration unneccessary.

The bedroom is a haven we turn to for rest and tranquillity, so choose blue tones of the sea and sky, paired with crisp shades of white – a classic combination – to evoke peace and calm. This chapter features vinegar painting and ragging; stencilling and the delicate art of freehand painting.

rest and

sleep

heart motif

materials

Wooden headboard

Pale blue emulsion paint

Household paint brush

Small self-adhesive stickers

Acetate

Black permanent marker pen

Craft knife

Cutting mat

Spray adhesive

*Red concentrated artist's
acrylic colour*

Square-ended artist's brush

Clear matt acrylic varnish

Varnishing brush

preparation

*Headboard should be
sanded, acrylic primer
undercoat applied and painted
with 2 coats of pale blue
emulsion paint*

For centuries, hearts, like flowers, have been used symbolically to decorate painted furniture, embroidered textiles and wood carvings. Hearts have such a nostalgic and romantic appeal that it is hardly suprising that they are as popular today as they have always been, and where more appropriate to feature them than in the bedroom?

The inspiration for the heart design on this wooden headboard comes from cross-stitch motifs found on antique bed and household linens. Traditionally motifs were embroidered in red yarns on white linen, so I have kept the red but for a modern slant, stencilled onto an ice blue background instead of white. Red and blue are neighbours on the colour spectrum and so mix well together but when used in conjunction with white, their brilliance seems to be heightened. Teaming crisp white bedlinen with this colour scheme shows off the red hearts to their best. As the heart motif is geometric, care is needed when cutting out the stencil. Practise stencilling on another surface first.

  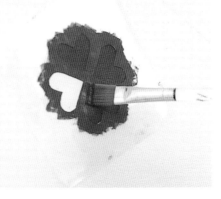

1 Put stickers on headboard

To mark the position for the stencil, put self-adhesive stickers in a random pattern onto the headboard. Make a copy of the heart template (see page 123), sizing it up or down as required. Trace onto acetate and cut out using a craft knife and cutting mat.

2 Spray stencil with adhesive

Lightly spray the back of stencil with spray adhesive and leave for 30 seconds until tacky. Position the centre of the stencil, tacky side down, over one of the stickers. Press the stencil on to secure.

3 Paint hearts on headboard

Using a square-ended artist's brush, fill in the hearts with red acrylic. Carefully remove the stencil and repeat steps 1 and 2 for the remaining stickers on the headboard. Allow to dry, then peel off the stickers. Apply 2 coats of varnish to finish.

country ragging

materials

Wooden bedside table

Masking tape, low tack

Vinegar paint (4 teaspoons cerulean blue powder paint and 1 teaspoon sugar dissolved in 1 tablespoon hot water, then mixed with 100 ml of vinegar and 200 ml warm water)

Large household paint brush

Thin plastic bag

Square-ended artist's brush

Tracing paper

Soft leaded pencil

Stencil card

Spray adhesive

Craft knife

Cutting mat

Ruler

White stencil paint

Flat oil-based varnish, extra pale

Varnishing brush

preparation

Table should be sanded, acrylic primer undercoat applied and painted with 2 coats of white oil-based undercoat. Lightly sand again

Vinegar painting is an early American wood graining technique with a charm all its own, specially devised for speed in covering large areas. The effect is not always recognizable as wood graining, but more as a fanciful allover pattern. The vinegar keeps the paint slippery, so if you don't like the initial effect you can simply wipe it off while it is still wet and start again. You can use many devices to apply the paint; I experimented and found that a thin plastic supermarket bag, when scrunched up, worked exceptionally well. You could also try crumpled paper, modelling clay or cloth rags. In general, a dark colour painted over a light colour works best, as seen here with this ragged bedside table: bright blue vinegar paint has been applied on top of a white base. Test a small area first with the vinegar paint, as you may experience cissing (where paint is unable to adhere to the surface and remains in tiny globules). If this happens, sponge the surface with whiting (see page 127), allow to dry, dust off loose powder and proceed as directed.

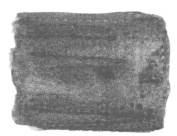

1 Apply vinegar paint to side panel

The painting has to be done in stages or the paint will dry before you have the chance to create the scrunched effect. Mask off the top edge of table all the way round and the inside edges of the legs (these edges will be painted last). Using a large brush, apply the vinegar paint with criss-cross brush strokes.

2 Scrunch painted surface

Scrunch up a plastic bag into a sausage shape. Dab this over the surface of the paint on the side panel before it dries. Use different parts of the bag for a varied effect and dab randomly. Repeat the painting and dabbing on the remaining side panels and top of the table. Carefully peel off the tape. Allow to dry.

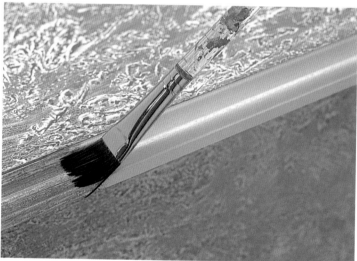

3 Dab top inside edge of table legs

Carefully paint and dab the four legs in the same way, making sure you dab the scrunched plastic bag into the corners and inside edge for an even, overall appearance. Allow to dry.

4 Paint top edge of table

Using a square-ended artist's brush, paint the edge around the table with the vinegar paint. While the paint is still wet, dab with the scrunched plastic bag as before. Allow to dry.

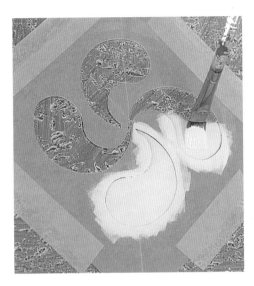

5 Stencil swirl motif

Trace the swirl motif (see page 123) onto
tracing paper, stick onto stencil card with
spray adhesive and cut out with a craft knife
and cutting mat. Find the centre of one side
panel and draw a cross to mark this. Using
strips of masking tape, fix the stencil in
place, making sure that its centre goes over
the cross. Fill in the stencil with white paint.
Remove the stencil. Join the segments of the
swirl by painting the gap where they meet.
Allow to dry and apply 2 coats of varnish
to finish.

storage trunk
simple initials

materials

Wooden trunk

Water-based satinwood paint in tan, pale blue and stone

Household paint brushes

Ruler

Soft leaded pencil

Masking tape, low tack

Tracing paper

Square-ended artist's brush

Fine-tipped artist's brush

Clear matt acrylic varnish

Varnishing brush

preparation

Trunk should be sanded, acrylic primer undercoat applied and painted with 2 coats of tan water-based satinwood paint

A personalized storage trunk would make a lovely gift for a wedding, a christening or a special anniversary. There is something unique about having your own initials and a commemorative date painted onto a chest or trunk. There are many old painted chests in both museums and antique shops, some richly decorated with beautiful designs and original motifs – these are wonderful sources of inspiration – and you could copy these designs or create your own. The trunk has a very modern feel to it; its beauty lies in its simplicity decorated as it is with a plain, wide band of colour onto which oversized letters and numbers are painted. I have included a template of a plain yet attractive alphabet and numerals for you to copy (see pages 74–77), scaling up or down on a photocopier to fit the trunk or chest. Don't feel bound to using the same tan, pale blue and stone colours suggested here, but rather choose tones and shades that tie in and complement the existing colour scheme in your bedroom or guest room.

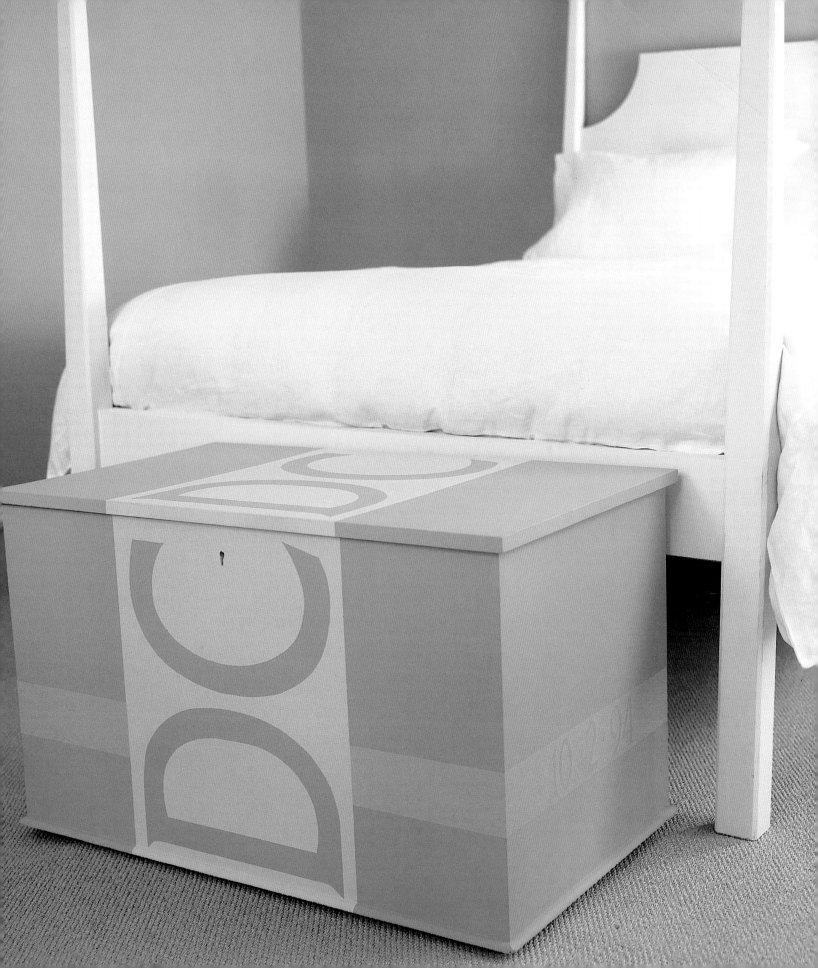

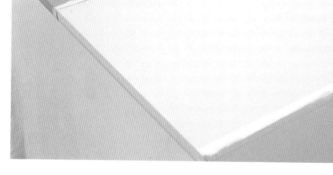

1 Mask off panels on top of trunk

Using a ruler and pencil, measure and mark out 3 panels on top of the trunk (the centre panel should be about 1½ times the width of the 2 outer panels) and mask off with masking tape. Using fingers, smooth down the tape to prevent paint from seeping underneath.

2 Paint outer panels blue

Using a household brush, paint the outer panels pale blue. Remove the tape. Draw panels on the front and back of the trunk to line up with the panels on top. Mask off and paint blue, as before. Remove the tape. Paint both ends of the trunk pale blue and allow to dry.

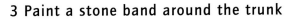

3 Paint a stone band around the trunk

Using a ruler and pencil, mark out and draw in a band around the blue panels near the base of the trunk. Mask off outside the pencil lines. Paint the band with stone paint. Remove the tape. Allow to dry.

4 Trace letters from template

Photocopy 2 letters from this page, large enough to fit in the centre panel on top of the trunk, and cut them out. Lay the first letter in position, tape tracing paper over it and trace the outline. Repeat for the second letter, on the same tracing paper, making sure the letters are equally spaced.

5 Transfer image of letters to trunk top

Take the tracing paper off, reverse it so that the letters appear back to front and using a pencil, go over the lines. Reverse the tracing paper again and tape it in position on the trunk top. Draw over the outline to transfer the letters to the panel. Remove the tracing paper. Draw over any faint lines. Repeat lettering on the front panel of the trunk.

6 Paint letters pale blue

Using a small, square-ended artist's brush, fill in the letters on the top and front of the trunk with the same pale blue paint as before. If your hand is not too steady, it may be helpful to mask off any straight edges of the letters before painting them.

7 Paint numbers for date

Repeat the tracing and transfering steps for the date, to fit in the stone band on the side of the trunk – the middle number should be in the centre of the band. Using a fine-tipped brush, fill in with the same pale blue paint as before, painting over the pencil lines. Allow to dry.

8 An important date

Repeat the date in the stone band on the other side of the trunk, making sure that the numbers and dots are evenly spaced, as before. Allow to dry. Apply 2 coats of varnish to finish.

friendship box
crested garland

materials

Wooden box

Concentrated artist's acrylic colour in pale blue, dark blue and indigo

Household paint brush

Black permanent marker pen

Ruler

White conté pencil, sharpened

Masking tape, low-tack

White Plaka paint

Square-ended artist's brush

Tracing paper

Soft leaded pencil

Fine-tipped artist's brush

Clear matt acrylic varnish

Varnishing brush

preparation

Box should be sanded, acrylic primer undercoat applied and painted with 2 coats of pale blue concentrated artist's acrylic colour

Small wooden boxes have endless possibilities for storage – jewellery, family photographs, important papers and documents, sewing kit or even as a place to put odds and ends. A medium-sized wooden box fitted with a hinged lid is best for this project. Here, I have painted the box with narrow blue stripes and then decorated the top with a dotted outline of a heart, enclosed by a delicate garland of white leaves and simple flowers. The combination of blues look sophisticated and the white garland adds charm and elegance. Don't be deterred by the number of steps involved in painting and decorating this box – it may seem complicated but the steps follow a systematic and logical order; the important thing to remember here is the sequence of taping then painting the stripes. I have recommended concentrated artist's acrylic colour for the stripes. Alternatively, you could use small tester pots of household paints, available from most DIY stores. The opaqueness of Plaka paint, for the garland, is perfect for painting over strong blues.

1 Draw lines on box top

Make pen marks at equal intervals along both lengths of the box lid and continuing down each side of the box. Using a white conté pencil and ruler mark out a central panel on the lid.

2 Put masking tape on box

Mask off stripes on the lid and around the sides of the box. Using fingers, smooth down the masking tape to prevent paint from seeping underneath.

3 Mask off central panel

Put a strip of masking tape on the 2 long sides of the central panel on the lid, making sure that the tape is on the inside of the white pencil line.

7 Edge box with a border

To make the border, put strips of masking tape around the base of the box, 1 cm up from the bottom and paint an indigo border. Remove the tape. Allow to dry. Do the same for all the outside edges of the box top, lid and sides.

8 Transfer image onto box top

Enlarge the heart and garland motif (see page 120) on a photocopier and trace onto tracing paper. (Draw registration marks to match up with the corners of the panel so the heart is central in the panel.) Tape the tracing paper face-down onto the box and outline the design in pencil. Remove the tracing and carefully go over the outline.

9 Paint a dotted outline

Using a fine-tipped artist's brush, lightly dot white paint over the pencil marks of the heart motif on the box top. Allow to dry.

4 Paint masked-off box blue

Using a square-ended brush, paint dark blue stripes on the top and sides of the box, going over the masking tape slightly, but taking care not to paint over the central panel. Remove the tape. Allow to dry.

5 Mask off central panel

Mask off the central panel by lining up strips of tape with the dark blue stripes on top of the box. Put masking tape all around the outside of the white line for the central panel. Smooth down the tape as before.

6 Paint striped panel

Paint dark blue stripes in the central panel, painting between the strips of masking tape. Remove the tape. Allow to dry.

10 Add flower details

For the stems, paint white lines over the pencil marks, add leaves and dot in the flowerheads. For the petals, lightly load the artist's brush with white paint and press the brush down into postion, twist it and lift off immediately to reveal petal shapes. Allow to dry, then finish with 2 coats of varnish.

contemporary style in classic

A treasured photograph of a loved one can take pride of place in a specially decorated frame. This wooden frame has been painted with pale blue and pure white checks, then lightly limed to mute the colours.

These bright blue antique chairs, through years of wear and tear, manage to hold an impressive stance with their high straight backs in a totally white room.

blue and white

The intricate fretwork of this white painted shelf is shown off in sharp detail when set against the vivid blue of the wall. An antique ceramic pot adds a happy note as it sits quietly on the shelf.

The bathroom has a dual purpose: a place for cleansing and a sanctuary for relaxation. A harmonious ambience is needed so the warming tones of pink are called for. This chapter describes how to crackle glaze a stool, add a burst of sunray to a shelf and symmetry to a peg rail.

simple

bathing

bath stool
beach stripes

materials

Wooden stool

White and pink emulsion paint

Household paint brushes

Ruler

Pink coloured pencil

*Masking tape, low-tack, about
2 cm wide*

Acrylic crackle glaze

*Satin oil-based varnish,
extra pale*

Varnishing brush

preparation

*Stool should be sanded,
acrylic primer undercoat
applied and painted with
2 coats of white emulsion paint*

A wooden stool makes a good resting place to pile on soft towels, soaps and shampoo while you soak away the hours and relax in a steaming hot bath. The stool can also be a temporary or permanent piece of bathroom furniture. Traditionally, crackle glaze is used to give furniture a distressed aged look, but here the pattern created by the cracked surface is used to create a contemporary look. The glaze is applied on top of a light colour and sandwiched by a dark colour. Then, as the top coat of paint dries and contracts the light colour shows through the cracks. The technique itself is simple, but for successful results instructions must be followed carefully. Apply crackle glaze evenly, directing brush strokes one way, and allow the glaze to dry thoroughly before painting over it. Humidity, temperature and the type of surface can affect crackle glaze, so it is best to experiment on a similar surface before embarking on this project; aim for soft, subtle and even cracks.

1 Mark out stripes

Using a pink coloured pencil and ruler, mark intervals the width of the masking tape along the 2 short lengths of the stool top. Repeat for the inner and outer sides of the stool.

2 Mask off stripes

Mask off stripes using the pink pencil marks as a guideline. To prevent paint seeping under the tape, rub fingers over the tape next to the area to be painted.

3 Apply crackle glaze

If you have not used crackle glaze before practise on another surface first. Using a flat brush and using brush strokes in one direction only, apply the crackle glaze over the stool. Allow to dry.

4 Paint pink stripes

Using a flat brush, apply the pink paint over the dried crackle glaze. When painting, take care not to brush over the area already painted or the crackled effect may spoil. The painted surface will begin to crack within seconds. Allow to dry.

5 Remove masking tape

Carefully peel the masking tape away from the painted edges to reveal crackled pink stripes. Apply 2 coats of varnish to finish.

peg rail shelf
sunburst design

materials

Wooden shelf unit

Pale pink water-based satinwood paint

Pink and dark pink concentrated artist's acrylic colour

Household paint brush

Tracing paper

Soft leaded pencil

Masking tape, low-tack

Square-ended artist's brush

Flat oil-based varnish, extra pale

Varnishing brush

preparation

Shelf should be sanded, acrylic primer undercoat applied and painted with 2 coats of pale pink satinwood paint

A splash of sunburst in chalky pinks brightens this pretty hanging shelf, providing practical storage for bathroom accessories, beauty and cleansing products as well as being a striking piece of painted furniture. A novel method of attaching the shelf to the wall – simply hung from pegs – introduces another element of interest to the overall Shaker look. The sunburst motif was adapted from a pattern taken from an old elaborately decorated patchwork quilt. I was struck by the sharp lines and geometric dimensions which seem to have an almost 3-D effect. You don't have to restrict yourself to decorating a shelf, as this versatile design would be equally stunning painted directly onto the wall or in the middle of a wooden floor. Care is needed to trace the motif accurately and to position it centrally on the shelf. Be sure to mask off the pencil lines exactly with tape so that each individual triangle and diamond, that forms the sunburst, is truly symmetrical.

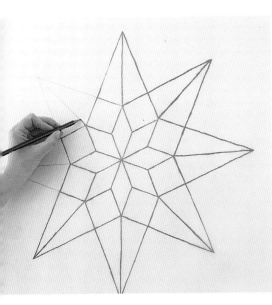

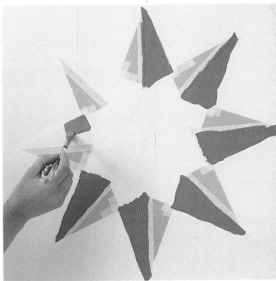

1 Transfer image to shelf back

Make a copy of the sunburst motif (see page 122), sizing it up or down on a photocopier. Trace onto tracing paper and tape it onto the shelf with the pencil lines face down. Using a pencil, draw over the design to transfer the image onto the shelf. Remove the tracing paper and go over the pencil outline with a pencil if the lines are faint.

2 Paint alternate triangles

Mask off alternate triangles around the outside of the sunburst, making sure the strips of masking tape are outside the pencil line. Using fingers, smooth down the tape to prevent paint from seeping underneath. Using a square-ended brush, fill in each masked-off triangle with 2 coats of pink paint. Remove the tape. Allow to dry.

3 Paint dark pink triangles

Repeat step 2 for the remaining triangles around the outside of the sunburst and fill in with 2 coats of dark pink paint. Remove the tape. Allow to dry.

5 Paint dark pink diamonds

Repeat step 4 for the remaining diamonds filling in with dark pink. Allow to dry. Apply 2 coats of varnish to finish.

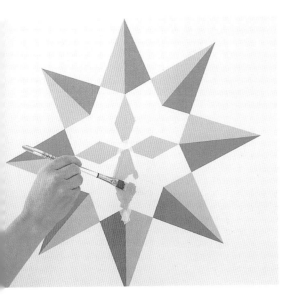

4 Paint diamond shapes

To mask and paint the diamond shapes in the middle of the sunburst, you will need to work on one at a time. Put strips of masking tape around the outside of one diamond shape, smooth down the tape and paint in pink. Remove the masking tape and allow to dry. Repeat the process for the remaining alternate diamond shapes. Allow to dry.

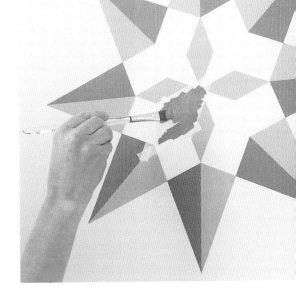

roman numerals

The simplest ideas are often the most impressive. Keeping this peg rail plainly decorated, uncluttered by pattern or embellishment, ties in well with the simple style associated with the Shakers. Also, in keeping with the Shaker ethos of functionalism, this peg rail serves a useful purpose of hanging damp towels from to dry after use. Soft fluffy towels, which have been appliquéd with matching numerals are an added feature. The symmetrical lines of the numerals above each peg is pleasing to the eye and a sense of order can be felt by numbering an object – it's also a fun way to identify one's peg in a large family or in a clockroom at school. You don't have to limit this design to peg rails, you could also paint numerals onto chairs, or bedroom doors – a tradition still seen today in Swedish manor houses. Photocopy the numerals from the template on pages 96–97, sizing them up or down as necessary, then trace and transfer onto the peg rail. Outlining the numerals in brown defines shape and enhances the finish.

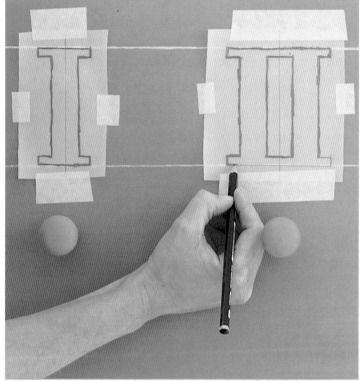

1 Measure and mark out panels on peg rail

Make a copy of the numerals on this page, enlarge on a photocopier, and trace onto tracing paper. Using a ruler and conté pastel, mark out a panel on the peg rail. (The width of the panel should be the same as the height of the traced numerals.) At each peg, draw a vertical line through the panel to mark the postion line for each numeral.

2 Transfer motifs onto peg rail

Using the vertical lines above each peg as a guide, tape the tracing paper into position, making sure that the pencil outline is face-down on the peg rail. Retrace the lines. Remove the tracing paper and using a pencil, carefully go over any unclear pencil lines.

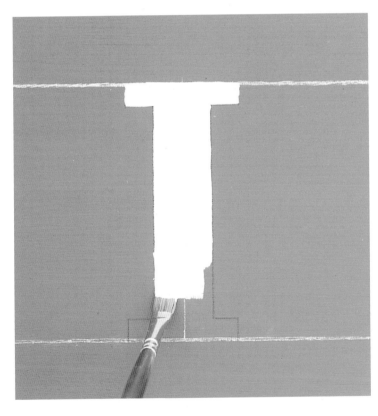

3 Paint numerals cream

Using a small square-ended artist's brush and working inside the pencil line, paint the numerals cream – the edges of each numeral when painted freehand will not be perfectly straight. Allow to dry. If neccessary, apply another coat of cream paint to the numerals. Allow to dry.

4 Paint a brown border around numerals

Outline the numerals in brown: paint a border around each one. Allow to dry. Go over the border again in brown paint to create a bold outline. Don't worry if the outline is not perfectly straight, as this gives character to the peg rail. Rub out the conté pastel lines. Apply 2 coats of varnish to finish.

white-on-white for freshness

In a pure white setting, carved woodwork will add visual interest and dimension.

A white-on-white interior always strikes an impressive chord in a bathroom where cleanliness is of paramount importance.

Assorted wooden containers are brought to life with the slightest dash of red.

An exquisitely crafted wooden panel stands guard in front of a less than attractive radiator. It doesn't obscure heat from the room as it can filter through the dainty cut-outs of the stylized flower design.

A traditional Shaker mirror is painted white, bringing it in line with the contemporary look of today.

A hallway creates the first impression for visitors to your home, so plan its style and colour scheme carefully. A theme, such as a woodland, using cool greens and aquas will invite your guests to feel welcome. Here, ferns have been silhouetted onto a table and several storage boxes have been stencilled with leaves.

halls and

entrances

hall table
forest fern

materials

Round wooden table

Pale olive water-based
eggshell paint

Household paint brush

Fresh sprigs of fern

Spray adhesive

Can of artist's blue spray paint

Flat oil-based varnish,
extra pale

Varnishing brush

preparation

Table should be sanded, acrylic
primer unercoat applied and
painted with 2 coats of pale
olive water-based
eggshell paint

The appeal of motifs drawn from nature is universal, whether it is flowers, leaves or grasses. Their attractive shapes are easy to transfer into pattern and look comfortable in a contemporary setting. Country woodlands and city parks are filled with the heady scent of fern and bracken and their uniquely shaped delicate fronds make an ideal template for a modern paint effect, which is so easy to achieve. All you need to do is gather fresh sprigs of fern and stick them down in a pleasing arrangement onto the table, then simply spray canned paint evenly over the top until the table is covered. Canned spray paints are available in a wide colour range from good art shops. Once the paint has dried, peeling the ferns off the table is incredibly satisfying and as your pattern slowly emerges, the slightly imperfect and fuzzy edges of the fern silhoutte looks enchanting. For dramatic impact, this paint technique works best as a dark colour sprayed on top of a light colour – the finished effect is quite ethereal!

1 Select sprigs of fern for table

Lay the fern on a flat surface so you can choose sprigs which are a good shape, flat and healthy. Include in your selection ferns of different sizes.

2 Apply spray adhesive to back of fern sprigs

Arrange the fern in a random pattern on the table top and edge. Remove one sprig of fern at a time, spray the back with adhesive away from the table and stick in place onto the table as planned.

3 Press fern on table

Using the palms of your hands, press the fern sprig down so that they are stuck as flat as possible onto the table top and edge. You may find that the thick stems of the large sprigs do not stick well to the table – don't worry if this happens; the result will still be successful.

4 Apply spray paint

Following the instructions on the can of
spray paint, spray the fern-covered table.
Make sure you spray evenly over the entire
surface of the table. Allow to dry.

5 Remove fern sprigs

Lift off the sprigs to reveal fern imprints.
Dust off any loose bits of fern. Apply
2 coats of varnish to finish.

stacking boxes
modern leaves

materials

Cardboard boxes with lid

Matt emulsion paint in lime-green, turquoise, cream, brown and pale turquoise

Household paint brushes

Acetate

Black permanent marker pen

White conté pastel, sharpened

Craft knife

Cutting mat

Spray adhesive

Square-ended artist's brush

Fine-tipped artist's brush

Clear matt acrylic varnish

Varnishing brush

preparation

Boxes painted with 1 coat of matt emulsion paint in a choice of lime-green, turquoise, brown or pale turquoise

A stack of assorted plain cardboard boxes can be impressively transformed into objects of desire, using a wonderful combination of colours and simple leaf patterns. Here, each box has a different leaf stencilled on top of a vivid base colour and then simple veins lightly painted in. You can choose to copy the oak leaf, chestnut leaf, or the branching leaves (see templates on pages 124-125), or pick out your favourite leaf design or botanical image from which to create a stencil. Tester pots of emulsion paint, available from most DIY stores, are great value for small-scale projects such as this one. These delightful designs can also be used to decorate small chests or trunks. For a festive treat, present your gifts in boxes that have been painted in Christmas colours and decorated with holly or mistletoe.

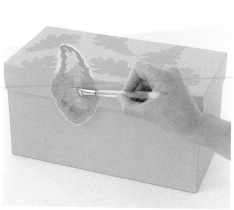

1 Paint oak leaf stencil

Make a copy of 2 oak leaves (see page 124) on acetate and using a craft knife and cutting mat, cut them out. Spray the back of the large leaf stencil with spray adhesive and leave until tacky. Lay the stencil, tacky side down, slightly off centre on the lid. Using a square-ended brush, fill in with turquoise paint. Repeat over the box lid.

2 Stencil side of box lid

To take the leaf design over the top edge of the box, put the stencil partway over the top of the lid and fill it in. Lift the stencil off and lay it flat against the side of the box lid lining up the edges of the stencil with the painted leaf on top. Fill in the stencil to complete the leaf design. Repeat steps 1 and 2 until the lid is covered in leaves.

3 Complete leaves near top

Remove the lid and turn the box on its side. Reposition the large leaf stencil over any incomplete leaves near the top edge of the box and fill in. Repeat steps 1 and 2 for the other sides. Allow to dry. Stencil in small leaf designs to fill the gaps between the large leaves on the lid and sides of the box.

1 Draw branch and stems

For the branch, draw a white pastel line slightly off centre from corner to corner on the box top. For the stems, draw lines at right angles to the branch line and continue the lines down the sides of the box.

2 Paint branch and stems

Using a fine-tipped artist's brush and cream paint, add fine lines over the white pastel lines to cover. Allow to dry.

3 Add leaves to stem lines

To paint the leaves, work on one side of the stem line at a time. Load the brush with cream paint and press it into position at the start of a stem. To form the leaf shape, as you pull back the brush, twist it off. Repeat along both sides of each stem. Allow to dry.

4 Paint leaf veins

Using a fine tipped artist's brush and the same lime-green as the box, paint in the leaf veins. Allow to dry, then apply 1 coat of varnish to finish.

4 Paint leaf veins

Using a fine-tipped artist's brush and the same turquoise paint as the box, paint in the leaf veins. Allow to dry. Apply 1 coat of varnish to finish.

define shape with colour

A simple yet elegant wooden cabinet blends well into the background. Its cool colour brings freshness and sublty to a hallway, creating a welcoming atmosphere to carry throughout the house.

Neutral colours work particulary well. Here a delicate shade of beige allows the items on display in this small cupboard to be the focal point.

The unusual shape of this upright country settle adds to its simple charm. Seafoam green woodwork accentuates the sharp outline against the white wall. A gingham blue squab and bolster give a softer feel.

Pick out furniture with clean lines and interesting features. Although verging on the puritanical, this bench sits comfortably on a terracotta tiled floor.

basic techniques

Following a few basic guidelines will help you to achieve paint effects that have a professional look:

Use the correct tools for the job You needn't buy much specialist equipment; more often than not you can use good quality household decorating brushes. You will only ever need two or three different sizes of artist's brushes, so it is worthwhile investing in good quality ones that will not lose their bristles. Other essential tools are a sharp craft knife, ruler, low-tack masking tape, permanent marker pen, white conté pastel or pencil, and acetate sheets for stencils.

Prepare the surface All wooden surfaces should be sanded down with sandpaper, dusted with a soft brush, wiped clean with a damp cloth and then left to dry. Wood is porous and, to prevent paint from penetrating into it, must be primed. In most cases I have recommended an acrylic primer undercoat, which is water-based and quick drying. Apply one coat of primer and allow it to dry thoroughly before painting on top with eggshell or satinwood paint. In general, a piece of furniture should receive two coats of paint, but you could get away with only one if the piece of furniture is not intended for heavy use.

Finishing a piece is as important as its preparation All painted surfaces benefit from being varnished to seal and protect the paint effect.

Finally, a good rule to follow with any paint technique is: practise on another surface first.

paints, glazes and varnishes

Paints have improved greatly over recent years, resulting in new-generation paints that are ecologically friendly, easy and safe to use. For simplicity, most of the projects in this book have been worked in a combination of four types of water-based paint: ideal for woodwork as it allows the wood to 'breathe'.

Water-based eggshell paint A quick-drying paint with a near matt finish, specially formulated for use on wooden surfaces. Available in a huge colour range in standard tin sizes, but no smaller than a 2.5 litre tin.

Water-based satinwood paint A quick-drying paint with a low sheen finish, specially formulated for use on wooden surfaces. Available in a large colour palette. Available in small quantities, ideal for use on small projects.

If wished, eggshell and satinwood paint can be used interchangeably.

Concentrated artist's acrylic colour Good colour range in small pots available from art shops. They can be mixed with other acrylics and glazes, and can be thinned with water, making them ideal for freehand painting and stencilling.

Plaka paint An opaque, traditional casein matt paint, available in small pots from art shops. Used for painting decorative details.

suppliers

paint suppliers and art materials suppliers

Brats
281 King's Road
London SW3 5EW
0171 351 7674
Specialist paint suppliers.

Craig & Rose plc
172 Leith Walk
Edingburgh EH6 5EB
0131 554 1131
Suppliers of specialist paints and varnishes.

B & Q plc
Head office: 0181 466 4166
Branches: 01703 256256
Extensive range of household paints and decorating tools and equipment at reasonable prices.

Crown Paints
01254 704951 for stockists
Major manufacturer of household paints.

Do-it-all
Head office: 01384 456 456
Branches: 0800 436 436
Stockists of branded household paints at reasonable prices.

Dulux (ICI paints)
Wexham Road
Slough
Berkshire SL2 5DS
Branches: 01753 550 555
Literature: 01420 23024
Manufacturer of a wide range of household paints.

Farrow & Ball
Stockists: 01202 876 141
Manufacturer of a wide range of paints in traditional National Trust colours.

Foxall & James
57 Farringdon Road
London EC1M 3JB
0171 405 0152
Large range of specialist paints and traditional brands of paint. Stockists of glazes, varnishes and waxes.

Green & Stone Ltd
259 Kings Road
Chelsea
London SW3 5EL
0171 352 0837
Specialists in artist's materials and drawing supplies.

Paint Library
5 Elyston Street
London
SW3 3NT
0171 823 7755
Suppliers of paints in a modern colour range.

Paint Magic
48 Golbourne Road
London W10 5PR
0181 960 9910
Specializing in equipment, tools, paint and materials for paint finishes: stencils, stamps and varnishes. Stockist for liming paste and crackle glaze. Mail order.

Pavilion Original Ltd
6A Howe Street
Edinburgh EH3 6TD
0131 225 3590
Fine specialist paints, glazes and stencilling materials.

Sanderson
112-120 Brompton Road
London SW3 1JJ
0171 584 3344
Own-brand household paints.

Annie Sloan Relics
35 Bridge Street
Whitney OX8 6 DA
01993 704611
Traditional paints including specialist pigments and paints.

Wickes
Head office: 08706 089001
Branches: 0500 300328
Household paints, decorating tools and equipment.

furniture and wooden accessoreis

IKEA
Brent Park
2 Drury Way
London NW 10 0JQ
Branches: 0181 208 5600
Reasonably priced bare wood furniture and accessories.

The Blue Door
74 Church Road
London SW13 0DQ
0181 748 9785
Swedish style furniture, accessories and textiles.

The Dining Room Shop
64 White Hart Lane
London SW13 0PZ
0181 878 1020
Dining tables, chairs and accessories.

Scumble Goosie
Lewiston Mill
Toadsmoor Road
Stroud
Gloucestershire GL5 2TB
01453 731 305
Ready to paint furniture and accessories.

Tobias and the Angel
68 White Hart Lane
London SW11 3AG
0181 878 8902
Untreated and unvarnished furniture, accessories and textiles.

Tim Chapman
2 Dunston Street
London E8 4EB
0171 923 9909
Mail order for unpainted cot-bed kits.

glossary

Acetate transparent plastic film for stencils.

Artist's brushes good quality brushes from art shops.

Artist's oil paint oil-based strong colours in tube form, used for tinting oil-based scumble.

Cissing paint will not adhere to the surface; remains in tiny globules. May occur when using vinegar paint.

Combing a paint technique that uses a combing tool, drawn over wet coloured glaze to create wavy lines, zigzags or swirls.

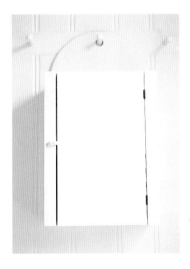

Concentrated artist's acrylic colour strong water-based paint that can be mixed with other colours, glazes or water.

Conté soft crayon-like pastel or pencil, used for marking.

Crackle glaze oil-based or water-based transparent glaze applied between layers of paint to produce a cracked effect.

Decorator's tape good variety of widths available. It is a low-tack tape, ideal for masking off and protecting painted areas.

Dusting brush (*see* Stippling brush).

Eggshell paint water-based and oil-based, available in a near matt finish in a large colour range. Used to paint woodwork.

Emulsion paint water-based mixed with a PVA resin and available in either matt or silk vinyl finishes. Available in a good colour range and often sold in small tester pots, which are perfect for painting and decorating small objects.

Liming paste available as an oil-based or water-based wax, rubbed into wood, then wiped off for a light bleached look. Works especially well on wood with an open grain.

Masking tape low-tack is the best type of tape to use, which will not peel away the painted surface when removed. As an alternative, use decorator's tape. Both are available from art shops. Essential for masking edges of panels and borders to be painted a different colour. Used also for attaching stencils.

Plaka paint opaque traditional casein paint. It is water-based with a matt finish. Ideal for decorative details and can be thinned with water.

Powder paint finely ground pigments in a limited range of vivid colours. Must be dissolved to use. Mix with water, sugar and vinegar for vinegar painting.

Primer oil-based or water-based acrylic primer applied on top of bare wood to protect it, so that the surface is ready to paint.

Ragging creates a scrunched, textured effect in a glaze using a cloth, paper or plastic bag.

Registration marks drawn on stencils and tracings to serve as positioning guides.

Rubber-ended brush with wedged tip, used for creating patterns in wet, coloured glazes.

Sandpaper available in various grades – fine, medium and coarse. Used to smooth down woodwork ready for painting

Satinwood paint a quick drying water-based or oil-based paint with a low sheen finish. Large range of colours available. Ideal for use on small items.

Scumble glaze oil-based and water-based glaze mixed with paint and used for broken colourwork such as graining and combing.

Sponge roller refill can be cut into a simple shape and used as a stamping tool.

Stencil card oiled manila card used for making stencils.

Stippling technique of repeated dabbing over wet, coloured glazes to achieve a grainy effect that eliminates brush strokes.

Stippling brush wide bristled brush with fixed bridge handle used for stippling. A dusting brush is a similar and less expensive alternative.

Tracing paper semi-transparent sheets of paper, used to copy and transfer outlines of motifs, patterns and templates.

Varnishes oil-based and water-based used to seal and protect painted woodwork.

Vinegar paint a homemade mixture of water, vinegar, sugar and powder paint.

Whiting ground chalk that can be used to prevent cissing.

acknowledgements

First and foremost my heartfelt thanks to Tabby Riley – a gifted,
sensitive and intelligent painter; she gave so much to this book.
Also many thanks to David Montgomery for producing consistently
beautiful images with unstinting energy. To Tim Chapman, who crafted
most of the furniture with perception and undaunted enthusiasm.
Finally, to all at Ryland Peters and Small who put so much time and
effort into this book, and thanks especially to Victoria Holmes and
Maddalena Bastianelli.

Many thanks to the following persons and companies for lending us
furniture and accessories, so that we could paint and photograph
them: The Blue Door, The Dining Room Shop, Pavilion, Sasha Waddell,
Scumble Goosie, Shaker, and Tobias and the Angel.